THIS IS OUR CITY
How the 2013 Red Sox
Kept Boston Strong

For the children of Waltham

by Melinda R. Boroson

illustrated by Gary R. Phillips

For information about permission to reproduce selections from this book, write to

Permissions, Forever & Ever Books, One Hollis Street, Suite 233, Wellesley, MA 02482

www.foreverandeverbooks.com

Book design by Michel Steingisser

ISBN 978-0-991-60200-1

Library of Congress Control Number : 2014937921

Printed in Canada

10 9 8 7 6 5 4 3 2 1

To the people of Boston—
and to people everywhere—
who face each day
with strength and determination.

This is Boston, the capital of Massachusetts.

This is our city.

Boston has a lot to be proud of.

A magnificent history.

Glorious traditions.

And sensational sports teams!

Boston fans have very strong feelings about their sports teams, ESPECIALLY the Red Sox.

Sometimes they jump for joy!

Sometimes they're down in the dumps.

One time, they had to be
very
very
patient . . .

for 86 YEARS.

At the beginning of the 21st century,
Boston baseball was going strong!!

The Red Sox won the World Series — TWICE!

In 2004 they pulled off an incredible triumph over the Yankees,
then swept the St. Louis Cardinals . . .

. . . and in 2007 they came through again
with an unforgettable sweep of the Colorado Rockies!!

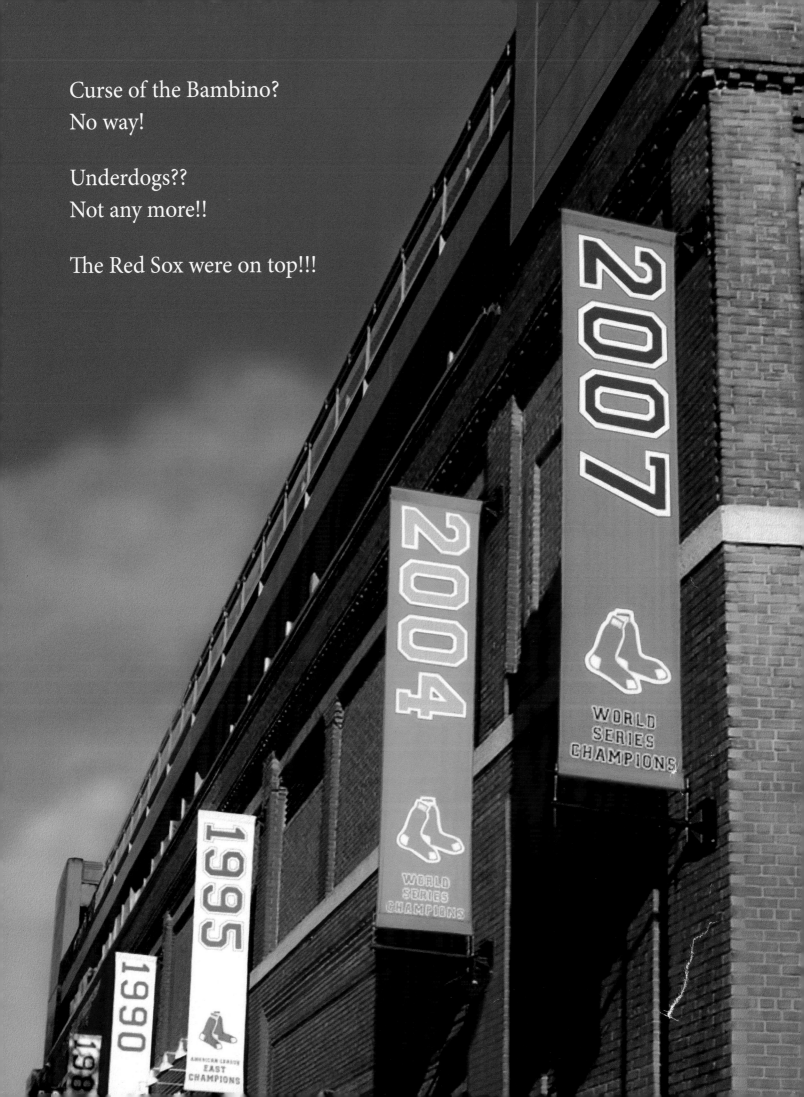

Curse of the Bambino?
No way!

Underdogs??
Not any more!!

The Red Sox were on top!!!

But then came 2012.

    The Red Sox were not on top any more.

        They were at the bottom.

            The VERY bottom.

AL EAST

	W	L	GB
NEW YORK	95	67	—
BALTIMORE	93	69	2
TAMPA BAY	90	72	5
TORONTO	73	89	22
BOSTON	69	93	20

Red Sox Nation remembered all too well
what defeat and disappointment felt like.

But 2013 was a new year, with new names on the roster
    Victorino
    Gomes
    Napoli
    Uehara
    a new manager, *John Farrell*

and a sweet 8–2 Opening Day victory
against the Yankees at Fenway!

And yet
for the first time in ten years,
there were empty seats at Fenway Park.

Even loyal fans didn't hold out much hope for this team.

But this Red Sox team kept going.

Bogaerts, Drew, Peavy
Their chemistry was growing.

Ellsbury, Buchholz, Ortiz
Their winning record was growing.

Saltalamacchia, Ross, Pedroia
Their beards were growing!

BOSTON RED SOX

DAVID ORTIZ

BOSTON RED SOX

JARROD
SALTALAMACCHIA

BOSTON RED SOX

DAVID ROSS

BOSTON RED SOX

DUSTIN PEDROIA

Every game was another chance.

To prove the doubters wrong.

To prove that teamwork can never be underestimated.

To prove that this Red Sox team was alive with grit and determination.

But the Red Sox had something even more important to prove . . .

They had to prove that,
    even after the bombings that had shattered lives
    and destroyed the joyous celebration of the Boston Marathon . . .

Fear would not win.
Despair would not win.
Hopelessness would not win.

Boston would win.

15

"THIS IS OUR CITY!" Big Papi told the world.
"This jersey that we wear today doesn't say Red Sox.

It says **Boston**."

When everything seems hopeless,
that's the most important time to keep going.

So the Red Sox kept going.

The Red Sox kept going
  And their hearts kept growing.
  Their commitment kept growing.
  And yes—their beards kept growing!!

All summer, all season: The Red Sox **kept going strong.**

They played hard against Tampa Bay
for the Division Championship.

And they won.

The Red Sox **kept going strong.**

They faced the best pitching staff in all of baseball,
the Detroit Tigers, for the American League Championship.

They never gave up.

20

And they won.

The Red Sox **kept going strong.**

21

And then, against all odds,
this team that, twelve months before,
finished last in the American League
in this city that, six months before, had felt crushed and brokenhearted

This Boston Red Sox team played in the 2013 World Series against the St. Louis Cardinals.

And they won.

The Red Sox kept going strong!

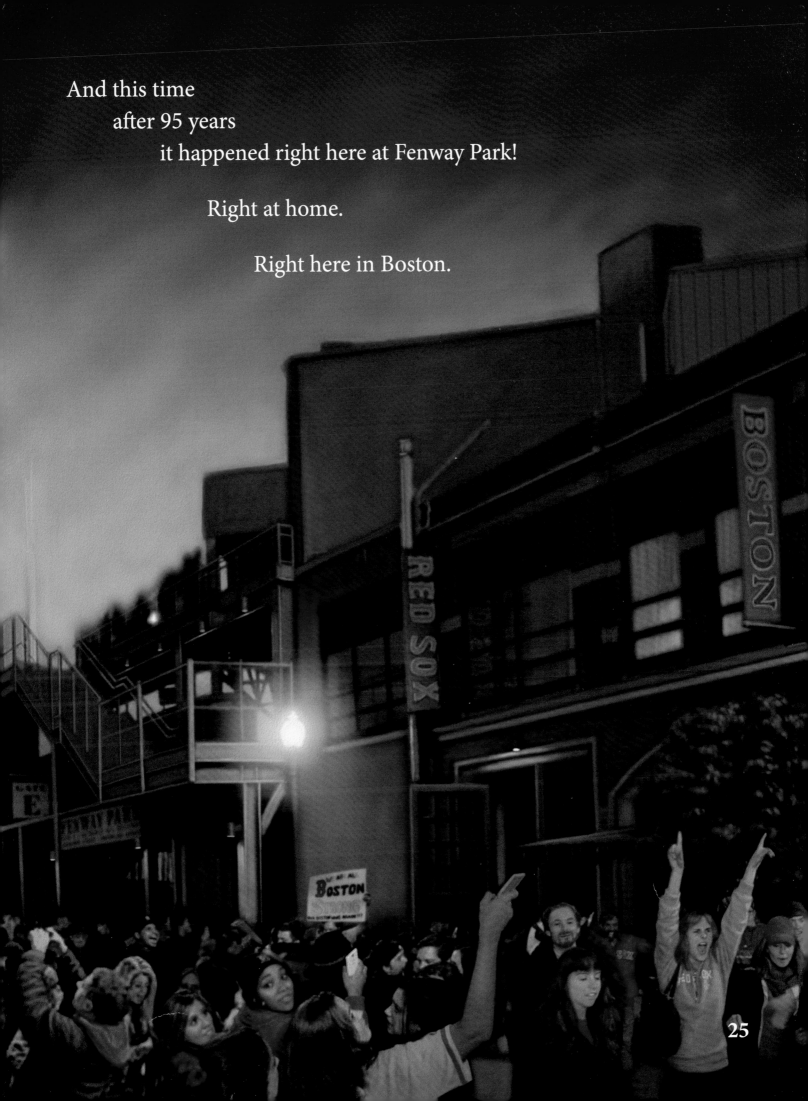

And this time
   after 95 years
      it happened right here at Fenway Park!

     Right at home.

      Right here in Boston.

So, this is Boston.

The capital of Massachusetts. The capital of Red Sox Nation.

Knocked down, but never defeated.

And always—ALWAYS—determined to **keep going strong.**

This is our city.
We will always be **Boston Strong**.

A Final Note...

A portion of the proceeds from the sale of this book will be donated to

THE ONE FUND
Boston / 2013

The One Fund Boston was established in April 2013 by Massachusetts Governor Deval Patrick and Boston Mayor Thomas Menino to help those families most affected by the tragic events that occurred at the 2013 Boston Marathon.

The One Fund Boston continues to collect donations to provide support for the families' needs and those of the broader community.

For more information or to donate to the One Fund Boston, visit the website at onefundboston.org or call 1-855-617-FUND.

GREYSCALE

BIN TRAVELER FORM

Cut By _Manuel Ovando_ Qty _18_ Date _12-2-24_

Scanned By_____ Qty_____ Date_____

Scanned Batch IDs

_____ _____ _____

Notes / Exception

_____

_____

_____

_____

_____